Dusseldorf
Travel Guide

Quick Trips Series

No part of this publication may be reproduced, stored in a retrieval system, or transmitted, in any form or by any means without the prior written permission of the publisher, nor be otherwise circulated in any form of binding or cover other than that in which it is published and without similar condition being imposed on the subsequent purchaser. If there are any errors or omissions in copyright acknowledgements the publisher will be pleased to insert the appropriate acknowledgement in any subsequent printing of this publication. Although we have taken all reasonable care in researching this book we make no warranty about the accuracy or completeness of its content and disclaim all liability arising from its use.

Copyright © 2016, Astute Press
All Rights Reserved.

Table of Contents

DUSSELDORF 6
- Customs & Culture 7
- Geography 11
- Weather & Best Time to Visit 13

SIGHTS & ACTIVITIES: WHAT TO SEE & DO 15
- Old Town (Altstadt) 15
- Media Harbour (Medienhafen) 17
  - Rhine Tower (Rheinturm) 18
  - Neuer Zollhof 20
- Königsallee 21
- Kaiserswerth 22
- City Courtyard Gardens (Hofgarten) 24
- Rhine Embankment Promenade (Rheinuferpromenade) 26
- Eko-House of Japanese Culture 28
- Benrath Palace & Park (Schloss Benrath) 29
- Art Collection of North-Rhine Westphalia (Kunstsammlung Nordrhein-Westfalen) 31
  - K20 Grabbeplatz 32
  - K21 Standehaus 33
  - Schmela Haus 34
- St. Lambertus Basilika 35

- BURGPLATZ 36
- PILLAR SAINTS 38

BUDGET TIPS 40

ACCOMMODATION 40
Rheingoldhotel Düsseldorf City 40
A&O Düsseldorf Hauptbahnhof 41
Hotel Plaza Novum Düsseldorf Zentrum 42
Hotel Madison Novum Düsseldorf City Center 43
Hotel Residenz City 44

RESTAURANTS, CAFÉS & BARS 44
Füchschen Brewery (Brauerei im Füchschen) 45
Luang Prabang 46
Curry 47
Naniwa Noodle & Soup 47
Carlsplatz 48

SHOPPING 49
Konigsallee 49
Schadowstrasse 50
Shadow Arkaden 50
Old Town 51
Carlsplatz 51

KNOW BEFORE YOU GO 52

- ENTRY REQUIREMENTS 52
- HEALTH INSURANCE 52
- TRAVELLING WITH PETS 53
- AIRPORTS 54
- AIRLINES 56
- CURRENCY 57
- BANKING & ATMS 57

- 🌐 CREDIT CARDS 58
- 🌐 RECLAIMING VAT 58
- 🌐 TIPPING POLICY 59
- 🌐 MOBILE PHONES 60
- 🌐 DIALLING CODE 60
- 🌐 EMERGENCY NUMBERS 61
- 🌐 PUBLIC HOLIDAYS 61
- 🌐 TIME ZONE 62
- 🌐 DAYLIGHT SAVINGS TIME 62
- 🌐 SCHOOL HOLIDAYS 62
- 🌐 TRADING HOURS 63
- 🌐 DRIVING LAWS 63
- 🌐 SMOKING LAWS 64
- 🌐 DRINKING LAWS 65
- 🌐 ELECTRICITY 65
- 🌐 TOURIST INFORMATION (TI) 66
- 🌐 FOOD & DRINK 66
- 🌐 WEBSITES 68

DUSSELDORF TRAVEL GUIDE

Dusseldorf

Situated in the northwest Germany, where the river Dussel flows into the Rhine, Dusseldorf is one of Germany's financial, fashion and cultural capitals. It is the state capital of North-Rhine Westphalia, Germany's largest metropolitan region, consisting of over 11 million people.

DUSSELDORF TRAVEL GUIDE

Dusseldorf is famous for its fashion and trade shows. Messe Dusseldorf, its fairground, is claimed to have organized and hosted close to one fifth of the world's premier trade shows. The city is also internationally known as a business and financial centre with the headquarters of five Global 500 corporations.

Over the last few decades, Dusseldorf has boomed; certain areas of the city have been developed by well-known architects, its economy has grown along with its population, and its reputation as an industrial powerhouse has been established.

Business visitors and fashionistas are not the only people who are lured to Dusseldorf. Tourists are often surprised with the culture, architecture, history and shopping on offer. Prepare to be dazzled by the city of Dusseldorf.

🌐 Customs & Culture

The culture in Dusseldorf is varied; from its highbrow art institutes and fashion shows, to its love of beer and celebration. The more highbrow elements owe their roots to an Elector, named Jan Wellem, and his Tuscan wife, Anna Maria Luisa de' Medici. The couple was a strong supporter of the city's first significant cultural activities.

Today the city boasts an extensive collection of theatres, museums and prestigious institutes, and the art, dance and music lover will love the city. Many of Dusseldorf's artists emerged from the Academy of Fine Arts, including Paul Klee, Joseph Beuys, Gherard Richter and Albert Bierstadt. Performing arts institutions in the city include the Deutsche Oper am Rhein (opera), the Dusseldorf Schauspielhaus (theatre) and the home of Gustaf Grundgens.

DUSSELDORF TRAVEL GUIDE

In contrast, as a stronghold for Rhineland celebrations and festivities, Dusseldorf hosts The Kirmes- Largest Fair on the Rhine- every year in July, an event which almost five million people attend annually. Held on the third week of the month on the left bank of the Rhine, in the Dusseldorf-Oberkassel district, the funfair features food and beer tents, vendors, amusement park rides and nine days of activities and events. Highlights include a drumbeat following opening ceremonies, a shooting tournament, masses in the St. Lambertus Church and a parade.

Another of the city's biggest cultural events is the Karneval, or Carnival. As much of the population is Catholic, carnival week begins on a Thursday and ends on Ash Wednesday the following week, peaking on Rose

DUSSELDORF TRAVEL GUIDE

Monday when an enormous parade fills the streets of Dusseldorf. The celebration mixes elements of circus and street party, with residents donning masks and theatrical costumes and taking to the streets. On Carnival Thursday, also known as Old Women day, women take to the streets; a woman in black storms city hall and "steals" the key, and women are known to cut men's ties and kiss passing men in commemoration of a women's revolt in 1824.

Additionally, Dusseldorf is also known for its beer. The historical district of Altstadt (Old Town) is known for serving a hoppy, old-style beer, whose brewing method comprised of using warm top-fermenting yeast prior to the lager brewing method. This style produced Altbier, or "old beer". The name was first used in the 19th century in order to tell it apart from the new pale lager that was

DUSSELDORF TRAVEL GUIDE

gaining popularity in the rest of Germany. Dusseldorf brewers would use the pale malts while retaining the old method of using warm fermenting yeasts. At pretty much any bar in Dusseldorf, you can savour the taste of an Altbier.

Like many other cities in the country, Dusseldorf organizes and holds a Christmas Market every year. Starting in late November, a variety of Christmas-themed events, activities, shops, vendors and sceneries are set up in different areas and squares in the city. Think lights, Christmas trees, sweets, gifts, ice rinks and snow. For a month, Dusseldorf is transformed into a winter wonderland, and spirits are at an all-time high. No matter your religion or spiritual beliefs, this delightful atmosphere is guaranteed to leave you with fond memories.

DUSSELDORF TRAVEL GUIDE

Dusseldorf holds a strong rivalry with Cologne, another city on the Rhine approximately 40 kilometres South of Dusseldorf. This rivalry, which includes competition and comparison of beer, carnival parades and sports, is considered to be "love-hate" in nature. While Dusseldorf's pride is Altbier, Kolsch is Cologne's progeny, so be sure not to order Kolsch in Dusseldorf and vice versa, or risk bearing the brunt of a joke and having scornful glances shot in your direction.

🌎 Geography

Dusseldorf is located on the river Rhine in the western part of Germany, close to Frankfurt and even closer to Cologne. It is comprised of 10 administrative districts, and each district can be further divided into several regions or boroughs. There are a total of 54 boroughs.

DUSSELDORF TRAVEL GUIDE

Dusseldorf is incredibly well-connected. Thanks to its position on the Deutsche Bahn rail line, over 300 regional and inner-city trains pass through the city's main station, Düsseldorf Hauptbahnhof or Hbf, each day. In total, over 1000 trains stop in the city daily. It is also part of a fairly complicated network of public transportation known as the VRR (Verkehrsverbund Rhein-Ruhr) which includes trains, trams, buses, subways and other lines; some local, some regional, some international. The S-Bahn, for example, a metro-like railway system, exists not only in Germany, but also in Switzerland, Denmark and Austria. Furthermore, the Central and Airport stations share connections with the national and European high-speed systems. It comes as no surprise, then, that the state of North Rhine-Westphalia is home to the densest network of autobahns in Germany.

DUSSELDORF TRAVEL GUIDE

Pricing is dependent on which mode of transportation by which you travel, and whether you choose a one-way ticket, return, or package. When traveling certain lines, for example, you will find that you will be charged for the amount of time. Trips under 30 minutes will be the cheapest. However, the frugal traveler may want to consider a Dusseldorf WelcomeCard. With purchase of this card, you have free access to unlimited public transportation within the city, as well as entry to many museums, discounts on city tours, boat tours, opera, theatre and numerous others. The card costs 9.00 € per individual for a 24-hour period, 14.00 € for 48 hours, and 19.00€ for 72 hours. There are reduced prices for families and groups.

DUSSELDORF TRAVEL GUIDE

🌍 Weather & Best Time to Visit

Like most of the lower Rhineland, Dusseldorf's climate is quite mild year-round. The winter does not see much snowfall, and average temperatures hover above freezing. Similarly, the summers are very tolerable, with daily means of approximately 18 degrees Celsius (64 Fahrenheit). The month of June sees the most precipitation, and July has the longest days.

Regardless of the time of year you choose to visit, Dusseldorf will be enjoyable. In the summer, the promenade along the Rhine is beautiful, Kirmes Fair celebrations are in full force towards the end of July, and those from hotter climates can escape the unforgiving heat. In spring, take part in the Carnival celebrations.

DUSSELDORF TRAVEL GUIDE

In winter, the Christmas Markets are not to be missed. Some patios are even open year-round, and dedicated beer drinkers can be seen drinking outside in sub-zero temperatures. In the fall, wander around the city and take in all of the beautiful colours which reflect off the Rhine and smaller waterways. In all four seasons, you're sure to be dazzled, as Dusseldorf is a gem which often does not receive the recognition it deserves.

DUSSELDORF TRAVEL GUIDE

Sights & Activities: What to See & Do

🌐 Old Town (Altstadt)

Though much of Dusseldorf was unfortunately destroyed by bombs in World War II, a few old buildings were left partially intact. After the devastation of the war, the city was forced to rebuild. In Old Town, construction was done with the goal of reflecting the city's historic plans and today, the Old Town really does look like a veritable historic little town.

In the Old Town, you can meander in and out of little shops, or simply sit at a café and soak up the sights and the people. At night, the district is turned into the renowned "longest bar in the world", as there are over 260 bars, restaurants and breweries within one square kilometer.

Home to the dark Altbier, the breweries, most of which are located in the Altstadt, are a must-see as they are an experience in themselves. Often, your first "Alt" beer is served without you even having to order it, and the same thing goes for the next when your glass is emptied, and the following 10. The Köbesse, or waiters, are constantly fluttering around with trays full of small glasses, empty and full. To keep track of your consumption, you are given a coaster and each time you receive a new drink, or food, your coaster is marked. To pay, bring your coaster to the bar. After you've decided you've had enough, this coaster-bill system doubles as a neat souvenir which is sure to bring back fond memories and laughs.

🌐 Media Harbour (Medienhafen)

http://www.duesseldorf-tourismus.de/en/guided-group-tours/the-medienhafen/

Dusseldorf's Media Harbour offers a view of several of the city's landmarks and contributes international recognition to the skyline. Hafen, which means harbor, is also the name of the district in which these landmarks are located. This area has undergone much development over the

DUSSELDORF TRAVEL GUIDE

years and now boasts several post-modern architectural marvels.

Along the banks of the harbor, you will find the Rheinturm, Gehry buildings, countless businesses, restaurants, bars, clubs, and many upscale apartment buildings. Most of the 700 companies in the area now have their headquarters in Medienhafen, justifying its reputation for innovation and trade. A walk down the "architectural mile" will dazzle you, though if you're not content with just looking, tours of the Media Harbour are offered through Dusseldorf Marketing & Tourismus.

Rhine Tower (Rheinturm)

20 Stromstrasse, 40221 Dusseldorf

Reminiscent of Toronto's CN Tower and Seattle's Space

DUSSELDORF TRAVEL GUIDE

Needle, the Rhine Tower's main function is to provide telecommunication to the city. Since 1982, after 2 years of construction, the tower has been carrying aerial signals for television transmitters as well as directional and FM radio. At over 204 metres high, the tower is the tallest building in Dusseldorf, and can be seen from almost anywhere in the city centre.

Special features include a light sculpture, a bar and restaurant. The light sculpture along the stem of the tower actually functions as a timepiece.

The design by Horst H. Baumann is the largest digital clock in the world, though most locals couldn't even tell you how it works. Wow someone by informing them that the clock is divided into three sections: hours, minutes and seconds, the top section being the hours and the bottom, the seconds. To read the clock, simply count how many dots are lit up in each section; if it should read more than 10, there will be two series of dots separated by a space.

The bar in the Rhine Tower, Günnewig Bar & Lounge M 168, is the highest bar in Germany. There is even a revolving restaurant at 172 metres, Restaurant Top 180. At both the bar and restaurant, prices are steep, but the view, experience and feeling of absolute extravagance are worth it.

For the budget traveler, the observation deck is open to public from 10 a.m. to 11:30 p.m. daily and offers a panoramic view of the city and all its landmarks. On a good day, even the city of Cologne is visible. It is free to enter the building, but the elevator ride up to the observation deck costs 4 euros per adult.

Neuer Zollhof

Stromstraße 26, 40221 Düsseldorf

Frank Gehry is the Canadian-born and American-educated mastermind behind so many famous architectural pieces around the world, including the Guggenheim Museum in Bilbao, the Walt Disney Concert Hall in Los Angeles, and the Neuer Zollhof buildings in Dusseldorf's Media Harbour. The latter, built in the late 1990's, are marked by broken geometry, wayward angles and curves, and reciprocal forms, all characteristic of Gehry's style.

Neuer Zollhof, or "The New Zollhof", consists of 3 separate buildings, each made with different and interesting materials. The middle building, for example, is clad entirely in metal so as to reflect the other two. They function today as office buildings, a role which seems much too bland for their eccentric nature. These buildings are the most photographed in Dusseldorf.

🌐 Königsallee

Königsallee, which translate to "King's Avenue", is better known by locals as simply "Kö". It is the country's boulevard of dreams, the busiest, most upscale shopping street by far, and the main reason for Dusseldorf's sophisticated reputation. Kö is located in the district of Stadmitte, and stretches one kilometer long, reaching the Hofgarten city park on one end, and running adjacent to the Altstadt.

DUSSELDORF TRAVEL GUIDE

In its centre lies a picturesque canal 31 metres wide lined with trees on either side. The water is fed from the river Dussel, originally in order to provide water for residents, and the trees are decorated with lights so that the nighttime offers even prettier sights.

After the trees were planted in the early nineteenth century, the boulevard was given the name "Kastanienallee", or Chestnut Avenue. However, after an incident in 1848, when horse droppings were flung at King Friedrich Wilhelm IV, it was playfully renamed and given its current title.

A far cry from the origins which gave the avenue its name, Kö now offers countless cafes, restaurants, exclusive shops, hotels, bank branches and offices. The Eastern side is entirely commercial whereas the Western side is quieter and more fitting for people-watching.

Whether you want to do some window shopping, credit card swiping, people-watching, or just be seen, Kö exudes luxuriousness and by default, you will receive a healthy dose second-hand fabulous.

🌐 Kaiserswerth

http://www.weisseflotteduesseldorf.de/

Kaiserswerth is one of the most ancient areas of the city of Dusseldorf. This historic district is located in the North of the city, next to the river Rhine, and contains the nearly thousand year-old ruins of the Kaiserpfalz castle.

DUSSELDORF TRAVEL GUIDE

The Kaiserpfalz, or Royal Palace, was home to the legendary Emperor Friedrich Barbarossa in the 12th century, but has had many occupants due to its strategic position on the river Rhine.

The town of Kaiserwerth was pledged by the emperor to the Archbishop of Cologne in the 13th century, then taken over during the Cologne war, then again by the Spanish in the 16th century, and again by the French and Dutch in the 17th and 18th centuries. Finally, many fortifications were destroyed, and the ruins are all that are left of the Kaiserpfalz today.

In the 19th century, the town became recognized for its deaconess clinic founded by a local pastor, where Florence Nightingale is known to have worked. In both

World Wars, the town was home to a military hospital, and in 1929, it became a part of Dusseldorf.

It's definitely worth the trek to the end of the city to see the ruins, imagine the history, and feel the charm of the little baroque houses. Regular tours are given by the Weisse Flotte company, with ferries leaving from Dusseldorf's centre. The excursion costs 12 euros per adult passenger.

🌐 City Courtyard Gardens (Hofgarten)

Pempelfort/ Stadtmitte/ Heinrich-Heine-Allee/ Inselstraße/ Jägerhofstraße/ Hofgartenstraße

40479 Düsseldorf

You can't walk very far in Dusseldorf without seeing or

DUSSELDORF TRAVEL GUIDE

crossing a park. However, the Hofgarten truly is the city's "green lungs", with almost 28 hectares of extensive meadows, trees, gardens, ponds and waterways. Shaped somewhat like a curved capital "L", it stretches from the Altstadt and Konigsallee northwest to the river Rhine, and East to Pempelforter Strasse, about 10 blocks away. It is a completely serene mix of nature and formal design.

Ironically enough, the peaceful park owes its conception to military events. During the seven years' war, conflicts had reached Pempelfort, which at the time lay outside the city's protective walls. Subsequent to this devastation, the Imperial Count Franz Ludwig Anton von Goltstein wished to restore harmony and order in the city. Therefore, in 1769, the oldest part of the Hofgarten was designed and constructed, making the Hofgarten Germany's first and oldest public park.

DUSSELDORF TRAVEL GUIDE

Not long afterwards, though, it fell to the French and was quickly returned. This presented a perfect opportunity to expand the park, so Maximilian Weyhe made plans to do so in 1804. The architect included in his plans a Hofgärtnerhaus, or Court Gardener House, to house himself, which is still there today.

The park is also adorned by many historic monuments and modern sculptures which complement the landscape elegantly, and a former hunting lodge which has also served as Prince Friedrich of Preussen's abode. Today, the palace, Schloss Jägerhof, serves as a Goethe museum.

If you find yourself in Dusseldorf on a particularly nice day in the summer, there is nothing more calming than a picnic in Hofgarten. And, regardless of the season, a stroll through the park will bring you to a Zen-like happy place.

🌎 Rhine Embankment Promenade (Rheinuferpromenade)

The city on the Rhine is home to one of the most beautiful promenades in Germany. Part of the rivalry with Cologne involves arguing over which side of the Rhine is the correct side to have one's promenade. Cologne has argued that the West side is the correct side, as the centre of the city is also situated on that side. However, in Dusseldorf, the sun shines all day long onto the promenade, which is on the East side of the river. On this side, you can also get a nice view of pretty little Oberkassel.

DUSSELDORF TRAVEL GUIDE

The esplanade is three kilometres long and stretches from Parliament to Rathausufer and to Rhine-Park, linking the Media Harbour with the Altstadt, the new with the old. It was constructed so as to be a completely pedestrian area lined by numerous coffee shops, bars and restaurants. Below is a tunnel buzzing with traffic, though along these serene banks, you'd never know it. With its sinuous pavement designed to mimic the waves of the Rhine, the embankment symbolizes the Rheinish culture and lifestyle in Dusseldorf.

Like Konigsallee, the promenade is the perfect place to see and be seen. The promenade is most enjoyable in the summer, when activity along the banks reaches a high. Locals and visitors alike are known to take strolls, have picnics, sit on the many benches or on the patios of cafés and restaurants, watch street performers, ships and sunsets or simply enjoy the picturesque view.

🌐 Eko-House of Japanese Culture

Brüggener Weg 6, 40547 Düsseldorf

Phone: +49 (0)211 / 57 79 18 0

http://www.eko-haus.de/en_index.html

Situated in the quarter of Oberkassel is Europe's first and only Buddhist temple. This pleasantly surprising find consists of a temple, Japanese gardens, kindergarten, library, and traditional house complete with tea room. The library offers a collection of Buddhist works, and the EKO-House even puts out two of its own publications: a scientific magazine entitled "Horin: Comparative studies on Japanese culture" as well as a semi-annual information leaflet, "EKŌ-Blätter".

The EKO-House plays an important role in Germany as it strengthens the cultural exchange and understanding between East and West. The location in Dusseldorf was chosen as the city boasts one of the largest Japanese populations in Europe. Here at the centre, the Japanese in the area are given the opportunity to nurture their traditions and customs while Germans are encouraged to participate and learn.

There are many events and festivities celebrated at the EKO-House. Of course, the traditional Buddhist celebrations are observed, as well as tea ceremonies, garden parties, musical and theatrical performances, reading and discussion circles focussed on Buddhist works and themes, as well as lectures and film presentations. Japanese art courses are also offered.

The cultural centre is open Tuesday to Sunday, 1-5 p.m. Entrance fees are 1.50€ per person, but if you would like a guided tour, it's best to call or email beforehand.

🌐 Benrath Palace & Park (Schloss Benrath)

Benrather Schlossallee 100-106 D-40597 Düsseldorf

0049 (0)211 89 21 903

http://www.schloss-benrath.de/en/portal_stiftung/bootportal.asp

Benrath Palace is a Rococo-style country cottage located in the South of Dusseldorf and originally built for Elector Palatine Carles Theodore. It was designed and overseen

DUSSELDORF TRAVEL GUIDE

by Nicolas de Pigage, the young French architect who received a prestigious education from the Royal Academy of Architecture in Paris, and operated for the nobility.

Construction took 25 years and was not completed until 1780. The Elector would use this house as a hunting lodge and summer chalet, built two hours away from his formal residence as dictated by tradition. The work marries art and nature in one wonderfully elegant union. Beside the Palace is an enormous park, nearly 62 square kilometres in size.

There are three wings, of which the Corps de Logis is the central building. In the West wing lies a museum of natural history, and The Museum for European Garden Art lies in the East wing. Exhibitions and concerts are held in the main building. The ensemble at Benrath is considered one of the most beautiful palaces of the rococo period, and has been recommended for designation as a UNESCO World Heritage Site.

Guided tours are given regularly, except for Mondays when the museums are closed. Credit cards are not accepted, so make sure you bring cash.

🌐 Art Collection of North-Rhine Westphalia (Kunstsammlung Nordrhein-Westfalen)

+49 (0)211 83 81-204

http://www.kunstsammlung.de/en/home.html

The Kustammlung NRW was founded in 1961 by the state government, and the first of this group of museums opened its doors 10 years later with the goal of educating

DUSSELDORF TRAVEL GUIDE

those interested and promoting influential artists, specializing in modern art. Through the years, it has expanded. Today, there are three venues, each with their own specializations and exhibitions, and with Mercedes Benz shuttle buses running between the buildings to transport visitors free of charge. Art enthusiasts will not be disappointed; the quality and immensity of the collection is extremely impressive. In total, the three venues provide more than 10,000 m² of exhibition space.

All wings are closed Mondays. Admission to K20 and K21 is 12 euros each, or 21 euros combined, and admission is free on every first Wednesday of the month starting at 6 p.m. Admission to the Schmela Haus is always free.

K20 Grabbeplatz

Grabbeplatz 5

40213 Düsseldorf

This wing was constructed and inaugurated in 1986. Its detailing is typical of the period, created by an architectural firm in Copenhagen, with a characteristic black granite façade. It highlights works of art from the 20th century leading up into the present. In 2010, an extension building for exhibitions was completed, adding another 2000 m² to the existing area, bringing the total to 5000 m². The existing area was also completely renovated. The buildings now feature an extensive library, state-of-the-art technology and two pillar-free exhibition halls.

DUSSELDORF TRAVEL GUIDE

K21 Standehaus

Ständehausstraße 1

40217 Düsseldorf

Standehaus was erected in 1880 but served as the Provincial Diet of the Prussian province of the Rhineland. Later, the building accommodated the Parliament of the Federal State of NRW until the year 1988. Following the relocation of the Parliament, the building remained vacant for 14 long years.

Then, in 2002, the current Ständehaus building was inaugurated as the second pillar for the Kunstammlung for modern and contemporary art in the presence of then-President Johannes Rau. This second building was the creation of an architectural office from Munich, and features a domed roof as well as an expansive sculpture garden on the top level. Though many fixtures were removed from the interior during its reopening, several original features were preserved, such as the outer façade and historic staircase. The building boasts four wings and three stories, totaling more than 5300 m² of surface area dedicated to exhibitions and galleries.

Schmela Haus

Mutter-Ey-Straße 3

40213 Düsseldorf

The Schmela house is the most recently acquired venue of the Kunstammlung. It was built by Dutch architect Aldo van Eyck and inaugurated in 1971 as the first building in the Federal German Republic to be erected specifically for the purpose of a private art gallery. Now under landmarks protection, the five-story building is made of gray pumice blocks and is characterized by interplay of interior (private) and exterior (public) exhibitions.

🌐 St. Lambertus Basilika

Stiftsplatz 7, 40213 Düsseldorf-Altstadt

(0211) 132326

http://www.lambertuspfarre.de/

A major Dusseldorf landmark is the St. Lambertus Basilika. It was built in the style of Lower Rhine Gothic with brick, and has one particular characteristic: a twisted tower. According to the legend, a bride dressed in a Snow White gown came to the altar about 100 years ago. However, as she was only pretending to be a virgin, the tower turned aside, ashamed. Legend says that if a true virgin appears at the altar, the tower will straighten.

Obviously, the tower has not straightened in over 100 years. The citizens of Dusseldorf, however, adore their twisted tower, and even after the war, they reconstructed it just as it was before.

The interior of the church is breathtaking, and as it is one of the architectural highlights of Altstadt, with its history and beauty, it is definitely worth a look when walking around the Old Town.

🌍 Burgplatz

This square finds itself at the old town limits next to the Rhine. It is named Burgplatz, or Castle-Square, because long ago in this same place laid the castle of the Earl of Berg, who later became a Duke. The castle was later reconstructed into a baroque palace, which then burned

DUSSELDORF TRAVEL GUIDE

down in 1872. The ruins were removed completely in 1888, and only a tower lay untouched.

Today, the tower still stands. There is a coffee shop on the uppermost level which offers a unique view of the Rhine and the ships passing by. Also found in the tower is the Shipping Museum (Schifffahrt Museum) which displays 2000 years of navigation on the Rhine.

The City Monument has also been built in this same square, a piece of art which was donated to the city on its 700th anniversary. It is a display of local history. Among the scenes depicted is the battle of Worringen, the signing of foundation documents by the Earl of Berg, a market scene and pope Nikolaus IV raising St. Lambertus Church to a monastery. Taking a few steps back, you will notice the horse riders on the left-hand side of the monument,

DUSSELDORF TRAVEL GUIDE

whose arms form the number 1288. This is the year of the battle of Worringen. In this battle, the Earl of Berg fought against the archbishop of Cologne; another reason for the rivalry between the two cities.

Additionally, you will find the Cartwheeler's Fountain under some old trees. The cartwheel is a popular symbol within Dusseldorf, and an old tradition. According to the legend, after returning victorious from the battle of Warringen, the Earl of Berg told the boys who were waiting for their fathers to show their happiness for the return of their fathers, and the boys began doing cartwheels. For this reason, the cartwheel is believed to have originated in Dusseldorf. Boys also used to do cartwheels down Konigsallee for change. Today, this tradition is continued with annual competitions of cartwheeling. The motto is "We will remain cartwheelers, however crazy the world may be" (Radschläger wolle mer blieve, wie jeck et de Mensche och drieve).

The square, which has received an award for being one of the nicest post-war squares in Germany, offers a small glimpse into the history and culture of the city with all its landmarks. It's certainly worth a visit.

🌐 Pillar Saints

All around the city you will find statues of characters standing on columns. The brainchild of artist Christoph Pöggeler, originally from the state of NRW, these statues represent the daily, sometimes mundane lives of the people which, when put on a pedestal, become noticeable and intriguing. There are nine statues in total: The Business Man, Marlis, Couple I, Couple II, Tourist, Father

DUSSELDORF TRAVEL GUIDE

and Son, Photographer, Stranger, and Bride. While touring the city, keep count of how many you can spot.

DUSSELDORF TRAVEL GUIDE

Budget Tips

🌐 Accommodation

Rheingoldhotel Düsseldorf City

Oststrasse 166, Dusseldorf, NW 40210

This affordable hotel is located in the city centre, within walking distance from Königsallee, K21 Standehaus, the

DUSSELDORF TRAVEL GUIDE

Media Harbour and the Old Town. It features satellite TV, balconies, complimentary internet access, and voicemail.

It has received a rating of 4.1 out of 5 and average prices for a single room are about 65 euro. This is quite a bit lower than most hotels you will find in Dusseldorf.

A&O Düsseldorf Hauptbahnhof

Corneliusstraße 9, Dusseldorf, NW 40215

+49 211 33 99 4 - 48 00

http://www.aohostels.com/en/dusseldorf/duesseldorf-hauptbahnhof/

This hotel is situated in the city centre, within walking distance to most landmarks. It is recommended by 95% of its guests. It features a bar and lounge area as well as a restaurant, wireless internet access, free cancellation, a library, billiards table, nursery and multilingual staff. The property is completely smoke-free. Most rooms are under 50 euros, and if you're really frugal, you can book a bed in a shared room for under 15 euros a night. With these prices, you can't really go wrong.

Hotel Plaza Novum Düsseldorf Zentrum

Karlstrasse 4, Dusseldorf, NW 40210

+49 211 177 60 0

http://www.novum-hotels.de/hotel-plaza-duesseldorf/hotel-plaza-information-duesseldorf.php

Located in the city centre, this hotel is within walking distance to many landmarks such as the Konigsallee, Old Town, and Media Harbour. The rooms are clean, spacious, gorgeous and modern.

DUSSELDORF TRAVEL GUIDE

The staff here is multilingual in order to accommodate the needs of visitors from all over, and the entire property is smoke-free. It offers Wi-Fi, satellite TV, and complimentary breakfast. Rollaway beds are available upon request. Prices are usually under 50 euros per night, except for weekends, and various discounts are available.

Hotel Madison Novum Düsseldorf City Center

Graf-Adolf-Strasse 94, Dusseldorf, NW 40210

+49 211 168 50

http://www.novum-hotels.de/hotel-madison-duesseldorf/hotel-madison-information-duesseldorf.php

For fewer than 50 euros, you can stay at this beautiful

DUSSELDORF TRAVEL GUIDE

hotel just East of the city centre. It is located two hundred metres from the city's main train station, one kilometre from Konigsallee and two kilometres from the Old Town. There are over 100 spacious rooms which feature modern décor, complimentary wireless internet access, satellite television, blackout drapes, and complimentary bottled water. There are complimentary newspapers in the lobby and a daily buffet breakfast is also free of charge. Hypo-allergenic bedding and a safety deposit box at the front desk are also available.

Hotel Residenz City

Worringer Str. 88, Dusseldorf, NW 40211

+49 (0) 211 550 488 0

http://www.residenzhotelduesseldorf.de/index_en.html

The Hotel Residenz City is very modern an extremely

affordable. Prices for standard rooms hover around 50 euros, but if you stay for more than 3 nights, then a discount is applied. The hotel provides free breakfast, a gift shop and newsstand, luggage storage and even a grocery store.

The rooms feature refrigerators, minibars, and beds with Select Comfort mattresses so you can get a good night's rest after your days of touring the city. It's not far from the Goethe museum, City Hall, Hofgarten or the airport.

🌐 Restaurants, Cafés & Bars

One could easily wander around the Altstadt, walk into any old bar or restaurant, and not be disappointed. The Schneider-Wibbel-Gasse lane is especially packed with eateries, many of them offering Spanish or Latino food. However, below you will find some detailed

DUSSELDORF TRAVEL GUIDE

recommendations of "musts" in Dusseldorf while keeping a budget in mind.

Füchschen Brewery (Brauerei im Füchschen)

Ratingerstrasse 28

+49 211 1374 716

http://www.fuechschen.de/

This traditional brewery restaurant is located in the Old Town and serves its own Altbier. Though the brewery is deceivingly huge, it's almost always packed. There's an outdoor patio, and several different rooms and areas inside. The atmosphere is incredibly and naturally vibrant, and the hearty laughs coming from the neighbouring tables are contagious. If you want an authentic experience, have an altbier and try the local specialty, Sauerbraten: vinegar-marinated beef with red cabbage.

Luang Prabang

Platanenstrasse 26, Dusseldorf

Phone: 0211 / 230 4275

http://www.luang-prabang.net/

If you find yourself in Dusseldorf with a yearning for Asian cuisine, then this is the place to visit. This Laotian restaurant has been voted #1 restaurant in Dusseldorf on several websites, and for good reason. The food is absolutely scrumptious, as are the cocktails, and the quality of the service is not easily matched.

DUSSELDORF TRAVEL GUIDE

The Laotian beer, Lao, a dark and blonde rice beer, is served, and the dishes are cooked as hot or mild as the patron wishes. Dishes are between 10 and 15 euros.

Curry

Hammer Strasse 2, Media Harbour

Phone: 0211.30 32 857

http://www.curry-deutschland.de/HTMs/curry0.htm

This restaurant offers an interesting twist on German cuisine, which has actually gained momentum throughout the country: curry. It has been accredited with actually being the first restaurant to offer this curious mix of cuisines in Germany. Try the infamous Currywurst; if you like sausage and curry, this is as close as it gets to heaven on earth. Prices are extremely affordable and the restaurant is open every day.

DUSSELDORF TRAVEL GUIDE

Naniwa Noodle & Soup

Oststrasse 55, 40211 Dusseldorf

0211-161799

This Japanese Noodle House located in the "Japanese Corner" of Dusseldorf often has a long line, so be prepared for a bit of a wait. However, the seats outside are heated in consideration of the dedicated patrons who endure the wait even in the winter. To kill time, a menu is also offered so that you may choose your dishes in advance.

The kitchen offers high quality soups and sushi at reasonable prices. Though it's well worth the wait, try arriving before 6 p.m. to avoid the long lineup.

Carlsplatz

http://www.carlsplatz.de/carlsplatz-marktplatz.html

Located in the Marktplatz square is this unexpectedly authentic farmer's market and gourmet paradise. It is absolutely one of the hidden gems of Dusseldorf. Buy your groceries here or sit and have a coffee or a low-cost lunch. The ambience is really tranquil and easy-going. For lunch, arrive by 11:30 to avoid lines.

🌐 Shopping

Konigsallee

www.koenigsallee-duesseldorf.de/

Whether you're shopping or just window shopping, Konigesallee offers the most exclusive shopping in

DUSSELDORF TRAVEL GUIDE

Dusseldorf and perhaps all of Germany. Many major luxury brands, such as Gucci, Louis Vuitton and Chanel, have stores on this street, as do many German department stores, including Seven, Kaufhof, and Koe Galerie.

Ko Boulevard is the epitome of extravagance and high-fashion. Prices are steep, but you can occasionally find a great deal, especially in the department stores. If you plan on taking on Ko, bring your credit card and plenty of energy and determination.

Schadowstrasse

Schadowstrasse is the more affordable and feasible alternative to Konigsallee. This boulevard is among the busiest shopping streets in the entire country, and actually is the street with the highest revenue in Germany. It offers less up-market shopping, department stores as well as more than a few unusual gift shops.

Shadow Arkaden

http://www.schadow-arkaden.de/

If you're visiting Dusseldorf in the winter and the weather outside is frightful, have no fear. Shadow Arkaden is an indoor shopping mall which will meet all your shopping needs. It has an eclectic mix of high-class and affordable shops, and familiar brands such as H&M and Zara are included in its almost 60 stores.

When your legs get tired of walking through this large mall, give them a break at the forum, which has cafes and restaurants ranging from a trattoria to a sushi bar. Considered to be the entrance to Konigsallee and

Schadowstresse, the heart-shaped shopping centre is also a venue for regular music events and exhibitions.

Old Town

Though it's known for its numerous bars and restaurants, the Old Town quarter does have a lot to offer in the way of shopping. Many small, local shops are located here, out of Konigsallee's pretentious reach. You'll find some great deals and unique knickknacks in the Altstadt, and when you've finished, become weary or thirsty, you don't have far to walk to a bar, brewery or restaurant.

Carlsplatz

The farmer's market in Marktplatz has not only a variety of foods and sweets to offer, but also popular artworks, flowers and various knickknacks. When you're hunting in Carlsplatz for a certain gift or souvenir, there's an added

DUSSELDORF TRAVEL GUIDE

bonus: cheap, delicious food that is so badly needed for fuel.

Know Before You Go

🌐 Entry Requirements

By virtue of the Schengen agreement, travellers from other countries in the European Union do not need a visa when visiting Germany. Visitors from Australia, Canada and the USA, do not require a visa, provided their stay does not exceed 90 days and that their passports are valid for at least three months after their stay in Germany ends. Travellers requiring a Schengen visa will be able to enter Germany with it multiple times within a 6 month period, if their stay does not exceed 90 days. They will also need to prove that they have sufficient funds to cover the duration of their stay. For a stay exceeding 90 days, non-EU visitors will need to apply for a temporary residence permit.

🌐 Health Insurance

Citizens of other EU countries are covered for emergency health care in Germany. UK residents, as well as visitors from Switzerland are covered by the European Health Insurance Card (EHIC), which can be applied for free of charge. Germany has excellent health care facilities, but emergency medical care can be expensive and will not be covered by the public health insurance of most non-European countries so health insurance cover should be obtained before leaving home. Visitors from non-Schengen countries will need to show proof of private health insurance that is valid for the duration of their stay in Germany (that offers at least €37,500 coverage), as a requirement of their visa application process.

🌎 Travelling with Pets

Germany participates in the Pet Travel Scheme (PETS) which allows UK residents to travel with their pets without requiring quarantine upon re-entry. When travelling with pets from another European Union country, your pet will need to have the correct documentation in the form of a pet passport. Certain conditions will need to be met. The animal will have to be microchipped and up to date with rabies vaccinations. Your pet will need to have had a rabies vaccination at least 21 days before your departure for Germany. If travelling from a high risk country, you will also need to submit the results of a Blood Titer test taken one month after vaccination and at least 3 months before your travel date. The animal needs to be identified either with a microchip or have an identifying tattoo.

DUSSELDORF TRAVEL GUIDE

🌐 Airports

There are two airports that serve the international gateway of Berlin. **Berlin Tegel Airport** (TXL) is the larger of the two and the 4th busiest airport in Germany. Originally a military base, it was used in the Berlin Airlift operation in 1949. Towards the end of the 1950s, it began to replace Tempelhof Airport. The other main airport servicing Berlin is **Berlin Schönefeld Airport**, (SXF), once the major airport servicing East Berlin. Frankfurt Airport (FRA) is the busiest **Frankfurt Airport** (FRA) is the busiest airport in Germany and the third busiest in Europe. Located about 12km southwest of Frankfurt, it connects visitors with the densely populated Frankfurt/Rhine-Main region. Frankfurt was home to the world's first airport and airline in 1908, but this was replaced by the current airport around 1936 when it grew too small to handle demand for air traffic. There are two main terminals, as well as a first class terminal used by Lufthansa. **Munich Airport** (MUC) is the second busiest airport in Germany and provides access to the region of Bavaria. It is located about 28.5km northeast of the historical part of Munich. **Düsseldorf Airport** (DUS) is the 3rd busiest airport in Germany and provides access to the sprawling metropolis of the Rhine-Ruhr Region. It lies about 7km north of Düsseldorf and 20km from Essen. **Hamburg Airport** (HAM) is the 5th busiest airport in Germany. Located about 8.5km north of the center of Hamburg, it provides access to the north of

DUSSELDORF TRAVEL GUIDE

Germany. **Stuttgart Airport** (STR) is located about 13km from the city of Stuttgart. It is an important base for Germanwings and provides connections to several European cities, as well as Atlanta in the USA and Abu Dhabi. **Cologne Bonn Airport** (CGN) provides access to Cologne, the 4th largest city in Germany and Bonn, former capital of West Germany. Founded as a military airfield in 1913, it was opened to civilian aviation in the early 1950s. **Nuremberg Airport** (NUE) is the second busiest airport in the region of Bavaria and provides connections between Germany and the Mediterranean, Egypt and the Canary Islands. **Leipzig/Halle Airport** (LEJ) connects travellers to Leipzig, Halle and other destinations in Saxony in the eastern part of Germany. Additionally it serves as an important cargo hub. Access to the southwest of Germany and particularly Freiburg, can also be gained via **EuroAirport Basel Mulhouse Freiburg**, (BSL) an international airport located on the border between France and Switzerland and near the border of Germany. It is operated by both countries with two additional German board members.

Airlines

Lufthansa is the largest airline in Europe and controls one of the largest passenger fleets in the world, consisting of around 280 aircrafts. It provides connections to almost 200 international destinations in 78 different countries across Europe, Africa,

DUSSELDORF TRAVEL GUIDE

Asia and North and South America. The group was founded in 1955. Lufthansa CityLine resulted from the absorption of the regional airline, Ostfriesische Lufttaxi by Lufthansa. Air Berlin is the second largest airline in Germany and the 8th largest in Europe. Condor Flugdienst is Germany's third largest airline and is partnered with the British group Thomas Cook, as well as Lufthansa, its parent company. It flies to destinations in the Mediterranean, Asia, Africa, North and South America as well as the Caribbean. Germanwings and Eurowings are low-cost subsidiaries of Lufthansa, currently being merged and integrated into a combined enterprise. TUIfly is an airline operated by the tourism group TUI Travel. It is based at Hanover Airport with bases at several other German cities including Frankfurt, Munich, Cologne, Düsseldorf, Saarbrücken and Stuttgart. TUIfly provides connections to 39 destinations in Europe, Asia and Africa. Germania is a privately owned airline which flies to destinations within Europe, North Africa and the Middle East.

Frankfurt Airport serves as a hub for Lufthansa, Lufthansa CityLine, Condor and Aerologic. Berlin Tegel Airport serves as a hub for Air Berlin and Germanwings. Berlin Schönefeld Airport serves as a focus city for EasyJet and Condor. Düsseldorf Airport serves as a hub for Air Berlin, Eurowings and Germanwings. Munich Airport serves as a hub for Lufthansa, Lufthansa CityLine, Condor and Air Dolomiti. Stuttgart Airport also serves as a hub for Germanwings.

Cologne Bonn Airport serves as an important European hub for UPS and FedEx Express. Additionally it is a hub for Eurowings and Germanwings. Leipzig/Halle Airport serves as a hub for Aerologic and DHL Aviation.

🌐 Currency

The currency of Germany is the Euro. It is issued in notes in denominations of €500, €200, €100, €50, €20, €10 and €5. Coins are issued in denominations of €2, €1, 50c, 20c, 10c, 5c, 2c and 1c.

🌐 Banking & ATMs

Using ATMs (Geldautomaten, as they are known in Germany), to withdraw money is simple if your ATM card is compatible with the MasterCard/Cirrus or Visa/Plus networks. Deutschebank is affiliated to Barclays, Bank of America, Scotiabank (of Canada), China Construction Bank, BNP Paribas (of France) and Westpac (of Australia and New Zealand), which means account holders of those bank groups should not be charged transaction fees when using the facilities of Deutschebank in Germany. Bear in mind that third party ATMs, however convenient, will also charge a higher transaction fee. Be sure to advise your bank of your travel plans and inquire about whether your bank card is compatible with German ATM machines.

🌐 Credit Cards

Most Germans prefer using cash when shopping and you may find the credit card option being being unavailable in many of the country's smaller shops, restaurants and guesthouses. Larger hotels and restaurants should accept credit card transactions. Shops will usually display a sign indicating which credit cards are accepted. The most popular credit cards are MasterCard, and its European affiliate, the Eurocard as well as Visa. Most German facilities are compliant with the new chip-and-pin debit and credit cards and may not be able to handle older magnetic strip cards.

🌐 Reclaiming VAT

If you are not from the European Union, you may be able to claim back VAT (Value Added Tax) paid on your purchases in Germany. The VAT rate in Germany is 19 percent and this can be claimed back on your purchases, if certain conditions are met. Only purchases of €25 and over qualify for a VAT refund. To qualify, you need to ask the shop assistant for export papers and this needs to be submitted to the Customs office at your port of exit, along with the receipt and a passport to prove residence outside the European Union. Customs officers will also want to inspect the goods in question to ascertain that they are unused. Once the export papers have been stamped, they can be sent to the shop where you bought the goods for a VAT refund. For a service fee, you can also get a cash refund from the offices of Global Blue, TaxfreeWorldwide or Premier Tax Free.

Tipping Policy

In German restaurants, you should tip your waiter around 10 percent or a little more if the service is excellent. This should be given to the waiter in cash, rather than left on the table when you depart. It is customary to tip porters in German hotels between €1 and €3 per bag. Tip your housekeeper between €3 and €5 per night and reward an unusually helpful concierge. Tip your tour guide 10 percent (although some tour guides may request a positive TripAdvisor review instead, as this translates to a cash bonus in certain tour companies), give your spa attendant 5 percent and round off a taxi fare to the nearest euro.

Mobile Phones

Germany uses the GSM mobile service. This means that most UK phones and some US and Canadian phones and mobile devices will work in Germany. However, phones using the

CDMA network will not be compatible. While you could check with your service provider about coverage before you leave, using your own service in roaming mode will involve additional costs. The alternative is to purchase a German SIM card to use during your stay in Germany. Until recently, Germany had four mobile networks, Deutsche Telekom (formerly known as T-Mobile), Vodafone, O2 and E-plus, but the latter two, O2 and E-plus have been acquired by Telefonica and are in the process of being merged into a single brand. A huge variety of packages for different types of usage are available from representatives and subsidiaries of each of these. Deutsche Telekom has two starter pack options - data only and voice and data - from €9.95, which includes €10 credit. For the same price, you can buy a Vodafone CallYa SIM, which also offers a basic €10 credit. You can buy your E-plus SIM card from gas (petrol) stations and retail outlets from €10, with a €5 bonus credit.

Dialling Code

The international dialling code for Germany is +49.

Emergency Numbers

Police: 110

Fire Rescue: 112

Medical Emergencies: 112

DUSSELDORF TRAVEL GUIDE

Master Card: 0800 819 1040

Visa: 0800 811 8440

🌐 Public Holidays

1 January: New Year's Day

6 January: Day of the Epiphany

March/April: Good Friday

March/April: Easter Monday

1 May: Labour Day

May: Ascension Day

May: Whit Monday

May/June: Corpus Christi

3 October: Day of German Unity

31 October: Day of Reformation

1 November: All Saints Day

25 December: Christmas Day

26 December: St Stephen's Day

🌐 Time Zone

In the winter season from the end of October to the end of March, Germany's official time zone is Central European Time, which is Greenwich Mean Time/Coordinated Universal Time (GMT/UTC) +1; Eastern Standard Time (North America) -5; Pacific Standard Time (North America) -8.

🌐 Daylight Savings Time

Clocks are set forward one hour on the last Sunday of March and set back one hour on the last Sunday of October for Daylight Savings Time.

🌐 School Holidays

German school holidays are not determined nationally and vary from state to state. The academic year begins early in September and ends in mid July. There is a weeklong autumn break towards the end of October, a two-week winter vacation that includes Christmas and New Year, a short spring vacation in February and a short summer half term vacation at the beginning of June. After the end of the summer term in mid July, there is a longer vacation that lasts until the next school year begins in September.

🌐 Trading Hours

German department stores are generally open from 10am to 8pm, from Mondays to Saturdays, while supermarkets are open from 8am to 8pm from Monday to Saturdays. Most German shops are closed on Sundays and also on Christmas, Easter and Public Holidays. German banks are open from 8.30am to 4pm from Mondays to Fridays. Most of the gas stations in large urban areas and near the autobahns are open 24 hours. Museums, tourist attractions, trains and buses maintain a limited schedule on Sundays.

🌐 Driving Laws

The Germans drive on the right hand side of the road as in the USA. A driver's licence from any of the European Union member countries is valid in Germany. If you are resident of a non-EU country, you may drive on that country's license for the first six months of your stay in Germany. You may need to obtain a German translation of your driving license. The minimum driving age in Germany is 18, but most car rental companies will require renters to be at least 21. Bear in mind that the majority of cars will be stick (manual) shift and that an automatic car may be more expensive to hire. You will need to have a Green Insurance certificate as well as standard on board emergency gear like emergency triangles, a jack, spare wheel and first aid kit. German autobahns or freeways are famous for imposing no speed limit, though you may find that variable speed limits are imposed on certain sections of the road, or a 130km limit may apply where safety and congestion is a factor. At the approach of a major junction or intersection, the limit drops to 80km per hour. In urban and residential areas, the speed limit will be between 30 and 50km per hour. You will need a special sticker or Umweltplakette (which costs €6) to be able to drive in designated Green Zones. A violation of this policy may incur a fine of €40.

🌐 Smoking Laws

Germany has banned smoking from all indoor public places including restaurants and bars, although it is usually allowed in outdoor sections, such as beer gardens. While some businesses have obtained exemption in states such as Saxony, Rhineland-Pfalz and Saarland, the regulations are particularly strict in Bavaria. Fines vary according to region, but can be anything from €10 to €5000. To buy cigarettes from a vending machine, you will be required to submit some form of identification.

🌐 Drinking Laws

The legal drinking age in Germany is 16, although minors can consume beer or wine from the age of 14, if in the company of a parent or guardian. They can, however, only consume and buy distilled beverages, such as whiskey and brandy, from the age of 18. In general, Germany enjoys some of the most lenient laws towards alcohol consumption and public drinking is mostly tolerated. Some places forbid the consumption of alcohol on trains and transit. Alcohol can be bought from a variety of places including restaurants, bars, grocery stores, garages and even newspaper vendors. Additionally the price of alcohol is the lowest in Europe.

🌐 Electricity

Electricity: 230 volts

Frequency: 50 Hz

German electricity sockets use the Type C and F plugs, which feature two round pins or prongs. If travelling from the USA, you will need a power converter or transformer to convert the voltage from 230 to 110, to avoid damage to your appliances. The latest models of many laptops, camcorders, mobile phones and digital cameras are dual-voltage with a built in converter.

🌐 Tourist Information (TI)

There are Tourist and Visitor Information offices in several of the larger German cities, where you can pick up maps and local travel guides to help plan your visit. The Berlin office is at 11 Am Karlsbad; in Frankfurt, go to 56 Kaiserstrasse; in Hamburg, 7 Steinstrasse; in Munich, 1 Sendlinger Strasse; in Leipzig, 1 Richard Wagner Strasse; in Stuttgart, 1 Königstrasse; in Hannover, 8 Ernst-August-Platz; in Dusseldorf, 65b Immermannstrasse; in Bonn, 131 Adenauerallee; in Cologne, 19 Unter Fettenhennen; in Nuremberg, 3 Frauentorgraben; in Dresden, 11 Ostra-Allee and in Dortmund, 18a Königswall.

🌐 Food & Drink

There are well over 1500 different types of sausage (wurst) made in Germany. These are divided into four basic types - raw wurst, cooked wurst, scalded wurst and, of course, the famous bratwurst, which can be found in over 50 regional varieties. Wienerwurst is a relative of the American frankfurter, but do not confuse the American frankfurter with the German one, a smoked sausage of pure pork which is regional speciality of the city of Frankfurt. There is also a good selection of raw and cooked ham, known locally as schinken. With 400 different types of cheese, dairy lovers will also be spoilt for choice, especially in the pre-alpine region of Allgäu in Bavaria, which produces the majority of the country's cheeses. A traditional German stew is eintopf, so named as it is prepared in a single pot. Enjoy Berlin cuisine with a delicious helping of eisbein, pickled ham hock served with sauerkraut or mashed potatoes. On the sweet side, apfelstrudel is a popular German pastry made with apples, cinnamon and raisins. If you are in Germany around Christmas time, spoil yourself with a helping of seasonal lebkuchen.

German drinking culture is synonymous with beer. The country has around 1200 breweries and more than 5000 different beer brands. In most parts of Germany, pale lager pilsner is the preferred beer, although wheat (weiss) beer is popular in Bavaria. Try a dark beer known as Altbier from Düsseldorf. As an after dinner digestive, Germans enjoy Schnapps, a clear, strong fruit-flavored alcoholic drink or herbal liqueurs such as Jägermeister and Underberg. Germany has some decent wine varietals from grapes that are grown along the banks of the Rheine and the Mosel. For a novelty, try an Eiswein (ice wine), a sweet dessert wine produced from grapes that were frozen while still on the vine. Apfelwein or cider is a popular alternative to beer and can be combined with sparkling water for Sauer Gespritzer or lemonade for Sussgespritzer. A local variety from Frankfurt called Speierling adds berries to the usual apfelwein. On the non-alcoholic side, Germans are also fond of fruit juice and mix this with sparkling water, especially apple juice. This particular mix is known as apfelschorle. Additionally, Germans love strong, flavorful coffee, which is hardly surprising since the coffee filter was invented in Germany.

Websites

http://www.germany.travel/en/index.html

http://www.german-way.com/

http://www.howtogermany.com/

http://www.germany-tourism.net/

DUSSELDORF TRAVEL GUIDE

https://www.deutschland.de/en/topic/life/mobility-travel/tourism

http://germanyiswunderbar.com/

http://wikitravel.org/en/Germany

Made in the
USA
Middletown, DE